ROME

Designed and produced by
Aladdin Books Ltd
70 Old Compton Street
London W1

*First published in the
United States in 1987 by*
Franklin Watts
387 Park Avenue South
New York, NY 10016

ISBN 0 531 10399 4

Library of Congress Catalog
Card Number: 87-50223

Design   David West
               Children's Book Design

Editor   Bibby Whittaker

Researcher   Cecilia Weston-Baker

Illustrator Rob Shone

Consultant   Patsy Vanags,
               Education Office,
               British Museum, London.

CONTENTS

GREAT CIVILIZATIONS

ROME

750 BC-500 AD

Simon James

FRANKLIN WATTS
New York · London · Toronto · Sydney

INTRODUCTION

The Roman Empire was the greatest in the history of the ancient Mediterranean world. At its height, it enclosed the entire Mediterranean Sea, and stretched from Scotland to the Sahara desert, and from Spain to Syria.

Rome united all these lands for the only time in history. It ruled an area that is today divided up among about thirty countries. This vast territory included a bewildering variety of peoples and cultures. The warlike Celts of France and Britain, the beautiful Greek cities of the Aegean, the ancient civilization of Egypt and the tribesmen of the Syrian desert were all governed by one man: the Emperor of Rome.

This book divides the story of Rome into four main periods. First, there is the rise of Rome from her obscure origins in the eighth century BC to mistress of the Mediterranean in about 40 BC. The second period, from 40 BC to AD 117, saw the Mediterranean united under Roman rule. The third period, from AD 117 to 230, was the climax of the Empire, a time of peace and prosperity which turned to chaos with civil war and foreign invasions. The last period, from AD 230 to 525, saw a new sort of Empire, struggling to survive against its foes. The story ends with the collapse of the Western Empire, and the evolution of the Eastern Empire into Byzantium.

Legionaries on the march
The soldiers who conquered Britain in AD 43 were heavily armed infantrymen. They had to be trained not only to fight, but also to build the forts and roads needed to hold conquered lands. Legionaries were Roman citizens who served as soldiers for twenty years or more.

CITY TO SUPERPOWER c750-40 BC

Rome began as an insignificant town in central Italy in the eighth century BC. For the first three hundred years, there seemed nothing special about her. Like most towns, Rome was a city state that fought with her neighbors. But, gradually, Rome beat all the other powers of Italy, from the strong Etruscan states to the north, to the rich Greek colonies in the south. In the third century BC she clashed for the first time with overseas powers, especially Carthage in North Africa. The terrible wars that followed almost destroyed Rome, but left her tougher and able to defeat anyone else in the Mediterranean.

By 40 BC, much of the known world had been turned into Roman provinces. But the generals of the conquering armies were thirsty for power, and began to fight for it. Rome, the superpower, became wracked by civil war.

Roman versus Roman
During the civil wars, Rome's oldest ally, the Greek city of Massilia (Marseilles) supported General Pompey. She chose the losing side. Below, Pompey's enemy, Julius Caesar, besieges Massilia.

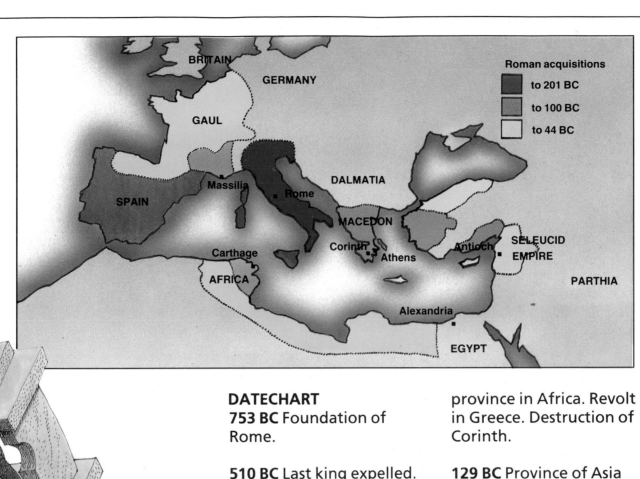

Roman acquisitions
- to 201 BC
- to 100 BC
- to 44 BC

DATECHART

753 BC Foundation of Rome.

510 BC Last king expelled. Rome becomes a republic.

4th to early 3rd century BC Rome becomes supreme in Italy.

264-146 BC Punic Wars.

218 BC Hannibal crosses the Alps.

197 BC Rome sets up provinces in Spain.

196 BC Defeat of Macedon. Rome controls Greece.

192-189 BC War with the Seleucid Empire. Victory brings Roman power into Turkey.

146 BC Destruction of Carthage; Roman province in Africa. Revolt in Greece. Destruction of Corinth.

129 BC Province of Asia set up in western Turkey.

90-88 BC War between Rome and her Italian allies. Rome forced to increase their rights.

63 BC Pompey destroys Seleucid kingdom. Syria becomes a province.

60 BC Pompey, Caesar and Crassus jointly rule the Empire.

58-54 BC Caesar conquers Gaul and raids Britain.

49-46 BC Civil war among Pompey, Caesar and others.

48 BC Pompey murdered.

44 BC Caesar murdered. New civil wars.

Myth and reality

According to legend, Rome was founded in 753 BC by Romulus, one of the twin sons of the war-god Mars. Abandoned near the Tiber River, the new-born twins, Romulus and Remus, were saved by a she-wolf (depicted in the statue of the Capitoline Wolf in Rome, shown in the photograph). When they grew up, the twins decided to create a city at the spot where the wolf had found them. But they quarreled and Remus was killed. Romulus became the first king of Rome.

The Republican army

Rome gradually became the most powerful of the many states in Italy, largely due to the organization and tactics of her army. The army was made up of Roman citizens who were called up for each campaign. They were divided into legions and grouped according to wealth, age and experience. The youngest were the lightly-armed *velites*, while the heavily-armed *triarii* were drawn from the experienced men.

Below, a young soldier says farewell as he leaves the family farm to join his legion for a campaign.

Roman Republican legionaries

Archaeology has shown that Rome actually began as a group of poor villages, in about 750 BC. These soon grew into a single town. At first Rome was dominated by its powerful Etruscan neighbors. But in about 510 BC the last Etruscan king, Tarquin the Proud, was driven out and Rome became a Republic.

The senate and the people

The Roman republic was far from democratic. Power was in the hands of the senate, which consisted of men from the most wealthy and powerful families.

The magistrates, who governed Rome and dispensed justice, were drawn from the senate. The most senior were the two consuls, elected each year. They commanded the armies.

Left, the consul is entering the senate house, escorted by his lictors. They carried bundles of rods and axes symbolizing his power to punish and execute people.

Ordinary citizens had few ways of resisting the senate. Peoples conquered by Rome had even fewer rights, and the growing numbers of slaves had none at all.

Elephants and warships
Rome's success in Italy led to wars with other strong states, especially the north African city of Carthage, which possessed a strong navy. Rome and Carthage clashed in Sicily in 264 BC.

The three terrible wars which followed, the Punic Wars, were some of the most savage in ancient times. Rome was almost brought to her knees by the famous Carthaginian general Hannibal. He took his soldiers and war-elephants by ship to Spain and from there led them over the Alps into Italy, and fought there for 16 years.

Despite enormous losses, the Romans eventually beat Carthage, even at sea. Rome had to invent new tactics, such as this boarding bridge which was lowered onto the enemy ship.

In 146 BC, Carthage was totally destroyed by Rome.

Power brings riches . . .

Rome also won wars against the powers of the Eastern Mediterranean. She was mistress of the known world, and became the greatest superpower the Mediterranean had ever seen. Soon she conquered much of the Greek world. The spoils of war made Rome rich. But her rulers were bad and often cruel. Here the Greek city of Corinth is sacked by Rome because of rebellion (146 BC). Its treasures and works of art were carried off to Italy and its citizens were sold into slavery, often to work for Romans.

. . . civil war and murder

The senatorial generals who conquered all these lands for Rome became very powerful men themselves, and their soldiers were more loyal to them than to the government. In the last century BC, several of these commanders fought the government, and each other, for control of Rome.

One of these men, Julius Caesar, defeated his rivals and took sole power. But in 44 BC a group of senators, demanding liberty, murdered him. Civil war erupted once again.

THE EARLY EMPIRE c40 BC-cAD 120

Julius Caesar's nephew and adopted son Octavian emerged as the unexpected victor of the civil wars following Caesar's murder. After the defeat of his last opponents, Mark Antony and Egypt's Queen Cleopatra in 31 BC, Octavian was master of the Roman world. He achieved two remarkable things. First, he brought an end to the civil wars, bringing peace and prosperity back to the provinces. Second, he held on to power for over forty years, and became the first Emperor of Rome. He was called Caesar after his adoptive father, and also took the name Augustus.

During his reign, many new provinces were added to the Empire, many cities were founded, and others were given splendid new temples and buildings. Augustus reformed every aspect of government, from the army to coinage, taxes and justice. He laid the foundations for the future.

Rebuilding Rome

Below, Augustus watches the final touches being added to the temple of Mars the Avenger in his new forum at Rome. He had sworn to build the temple when he had avenged the murder of his adoptive father, Julius Caesar. Augustus was a great builder, and introduced the lavish use of marble to Rome. He claimed that he found Rome a city of brick, and left it a city of marble.

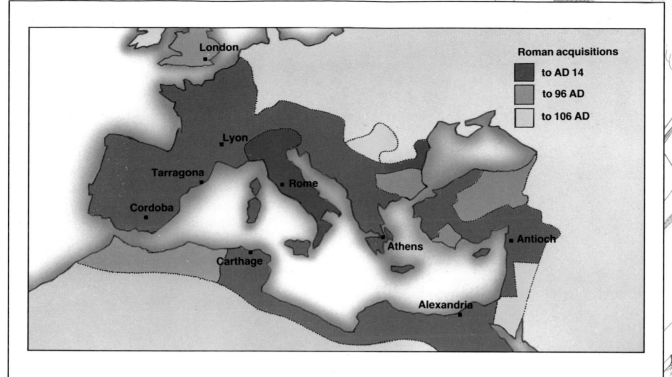

Roman acquisitions
- to AD 14
- to 96 AD
- to 106 AD

DATECHART

43 BC Mark Antony, Octavian and Lepidus jointly rule the Empire.

42 BC Civil war. Caesar's assassins, Brutus and Cassius, are killed.

31 BC War between Mark Antony and Octavian. Victory for Octavian at battle of Actium.

30 BC Suicide of Antony and Cleopatra in Egypt. Rome takes Egypt.

27 BC Octavian becomes Augustus, the first Emperor.

16-6 BC Conquest of Switzerland, Austria and Hungary.

AD 14 Death of Augustus.

AD 41-54 The reign of Claudius.

AD 43 Conquest of southern Britain.

AD 54-68 The reign of Nero.

AD 69-79 The reign of Vespasian.

AD 79 Eruption of Mount Vesuvius buries Pompeii.

AD 98-117 The reign of Trajan.

AD 101-106 Conquest of Dacia (Rumania).

AD 114-117 Parthian War. Attempt to conquer Mesopotamia (Iraq).

The first Emperor

Augustus was a very clever politician. Although he had sole power, he was careful not to upset the senate. He lived a very modest life, and purposely behaved like a Roman magistrate rather than a king. Here, acting as High Priest, he is sacrificing to the gods. Behind this public face, however, Augustus was building a new imperial government that was to last 300 years.

A day at the games

Games were held on many religious festivals. They consisted of theatrical performances, chariot races or exciting shows at the amphitheater.

In the great oval arena of the amphitheater, wild beast "hunts" were staged. There were also executions and fights between gladiators, often to the death. There were a few women gladiators, like these. Most gladiators were slaves or criminals. If they survived, they sometimes won their freedom.

The life of the rich

Here, a wealthy senator is giving a dinner party. The guests eat lying down, while domestic slaves bring more splendid dishes. Romans loved food; they had at least 17 ways of cooking suckling pig! But not all dinner parties were orgies. At this one, the guests are being entertained by a Greek slave, reading poems and passages from famous writers. Such well-educated slaves were very valuable and sometimes were treated as members of the family. They were often freed and a few were even adopted by former owners.

The most popular games were the chariot races. In Rome there were four teams: the Reds, Whites, Blues and Greens. They each had their stars and fans, rather like modern sports teams.

Today, many Roman amphitheaters, such as the one in the photograph in France, are still used for bullfights.

The bustling towns

Most of the Empire was made up of city states, towns with their dependent areas of farmland. Roman life was centered in towns, like Pompeii, shown in the illustration below as it was, and in the photograph as it remains today. Towns were divided into blocks by a grid or network of paved streets. Some blocks were given over to temples, public baths and the forum (the central marketplace, town hall and courts). But most blocks were patchworks of small shops, the housing of the poor and the mansions of the rich.

Roman children

Growing up was very different for rich and poor children. Here the son of a wealthy family is about to go off to school, accompanied by his pedagogue, or tutor (an educated Greek slave). It was thought that girls did not need to go to school. Children of poor families got no education at all. They had to go out to work instead.

The public baths

The baths were not just for keeping clean; they were important meeting places, like the forum. Better-off Roman men would spend the afternoon in these bustling, noisy places (women bathed earlier). After exercising, they went into the hot chamber to sweat the dirt from the pores of the skin (soap was known, but a little-used luxury). After a dip, and drying off, people might linger in the yard, chatting to friends and enjoying the sunshine. They might watch ball games, or buy snacks from vendors.

THE ROMAN PEACE cAD 120-c230

While it reduced the freedom of many peoples, the Roman Empire generally brought peace and security to the territories it conquered. Many people were probably better off, and shared in the growing prosperity of the Roman world.

When the great soldier-emperor Trajan died in AD 117, the era of expansion came to an end. His successor, Hadrian, did not go on wars of conquest, even though he was an experienced soldier. Instead, he spent much of his reign traveling through the Empire, inspecting the provinces and the armies which defended the imperial peace against attack or rebellion.

For most of the rest of the second century, the Mediterranean world was politically united, and at peace, for the first and last time in history. This was a "golden age" of relative happiness and prosperity, long to be remembered.

Planning Hadrian's Wall
Hadrian visited Britain in AD 122, and while there gave orders for the construction of the great wall. Below, the Emperor and his engineers discuss the line the wall will take, from a hill overlooking the fort of Vindolanda. Eighty Roman miles long, Hadrian's Wall ran from Newcastle to Carlisle. Much of it can still be seen today.

Provinces and frontiers of the Roman Empire

1 BRITANNIA	22 MACEDONIA
2 GERMANIA INFERIOR	23 EPIRUS
3 GERMANIA SUPERIOR	24 ACHAEA
4 GALLIA BELGICA	25 ASIA
5 GALLIA LUGDUNENSIS	26 LYCIA AND PAMPHYLIA
6 AQUITANIA	27 GALATIA
7 TARRACONENSIS	28 CAPPADOCIA
8 LUSITANIA	29 CILICIA
9 BAETICA	30 ASSYRIA
10 NARBONENSIS	31 JUDAEA
11 ALPES MARITIMAE	32 ARABIA
12 ALPES COTTIAE	33 CYPRUS
13 ALPES POENINAE	34 AEGYPTUS
14 RHAETIA	35 CYRENAICA
15 NORICUM	36 CRETA
16 PANNONIA	37 AFRICA
17 DALMATIA	38 SICILIA
18 MOESIA SUPERIOR	39 SARDINIA
19 MOESIA INFERIOR	40 CORSICA
20 DACIA	41 MAURETANIA CAESARIENSIS
21 THRACIA	42 MAURETANIA TINGITANA

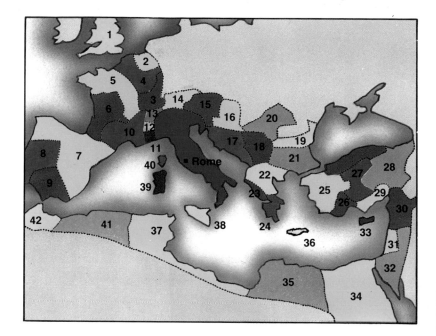

DATECHART

AD 117-138 The reign of Hadrian.

117 Hadrian abandons Mesopotamia.

121-126 Hadrian's first tour of the provinces: Greece, Turkey and the West.

122 Hadrian in Britain.

120s Building of Hadrian's Wall.

129-134 Hadrian's second tour: Egypt and the other Eastern provinces.

138-161 Antoninus Pius. His reign is remembered as a golden age of peace and plenty.

161-180 Marcus Aurelius, the "philosopher king."

161-166 Parthian War.

166 Plague spreads across the Empire. Roman envoys or merchants reach China.

167-175 Marcomannic Wars; Germans briefly break through into Italy.

180-192 The reign of Commodus.

193-7 Civil war. Provincial governors fight for the throne.

193-211 Severus founds a new dynasty, and embarks on new conquests.

195-199 Parthian War. Severus conquers part of Mesopotamia.

208-11 War in Scotland. Severus dies at York.

212 Roman citizenship for almost everyone in the Empire.

227 Parthia overthrown by Sassanid Persia.

A mosaic of peoples

The Empire was made up of peoples of many colors, cultures and languages. Most wealthy people eventually dressed in the Greek or Roman style.

1. Dacian (from modern Rumania)
2. Celtic couple (from Britain or Gaul)
3. Numidian (from North Africa)
4. Wealthy Roman
5. Greek
6. Wealthy Syrian woman
7. Jewish priest
8. Wealthy Palmyrene woman (from Palmyra in Jordan)

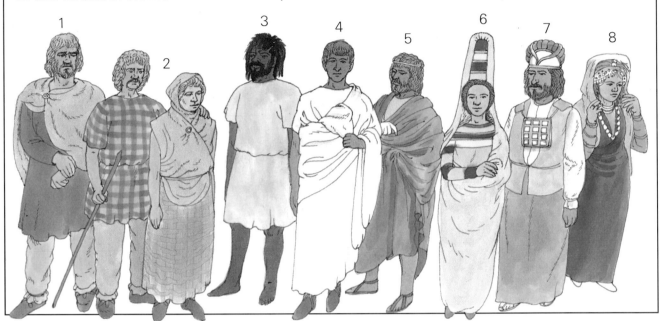

The rich become Romans

A wealthy Romano-British landowner rides out from his fine villa to see how the harvest is going. The tenant farmer and his family are British peasants not much affected by the Roman conquest. They still live very much like their Iron Age ancestors. The landowner lives like a Roman, and may be a Roman citizen, even though his ancestors were probably Britons.

Building – large and small

The Romans were excellent builders, especially in concrete, which they invented, and in brick.

Here we see the construction of a fine town house, and the installation of new drains.

Many Roman towns had piped water supplies and proper sewers.

The stone building beyond will have underfloor heating; hot air from a fire will circulate between the brick floor supports. On top of the floor structure, a mosaic of colored stones is being laid (inset). Mosaics were very expensive.

It took several years, and many thousands of tons of mortar and stone to build Hadrian's Wall, shown in the photograph below.

Arteries of the Empire

Having conquered an area, one of the first things the Roman army did was to build roads to let the troops move about quickly. These roads also made the movement of people and goods much easier, and helped to tie the Empire together in a political and economic network. Many Roman roads are still in use today. Some involved major works of engineering, such as this bridge at Alcantara in Spain. It still carries traffic, more than 1,800 years after it was built.

Ships and cargoes

The roads carried much of the growing trade of the Empire in the first century AD, but the cheapest way of moving goods was by water. Great ships sailed across the Mediterranean, carrying jars of wine, olive oil, and fish sauce, and also many other goods. At Alexandria in the Nile delta (below), Egyptian grain was put on freighters bound for Rome. Most of the bread baked in Rome was made from Egyptian wheat.

Camels and cults

A caravan carrying Chinese silk and other luxuries passes through the desert city of Jerash (in Jordan), past the temple of the Greek god Zeus.

Ideas, as well as goods, traveled across the Empire. By the third century, educated people from Britain to Syria all spoke Greek, or Latin, or both. Religions also spread across the Roman world. Greek cults, long known in the Middle East, now spread as far to the northwest as Britain and so did many religions, including Christianity.

A world of many gods

Most of the many religions of the Empire existed happily side by side. Most people believed that there were many gods, and Romans thought it was right to worship the gods of the peoples they conquered. They often identified local gods with their Roman gods, like Mars. This led to mixing of religions. Shown here are some Romanized Britons sacrificing to a Celtic god identified with the Roman god Mercury. Their temple is a British type built using Roman methods.

FIGHTING FOR SURVIVAL AD 230-527

For much of the third century AD, the Empire was wracked by war. There were massive invasions by Germans from the north, and a new enemy, Persia, from the east. Roman generals also fought each other for the throne. There was an economic crisis. The Empire began to break up.

But then, in the nick of time, a series of soldier-emperors arose, drove out the invaders and reunited the Empire. The greatest of these men was Diocletian, who from AD 284 to 305 brought security at last. But the cost was great. The Empire was besieged, and was only kept going by force. The people in the provinces found it hard to supply the huge armies needed to keep the barbarians out. The fourth century emperors, almost all Christians, usually managed to hold the invaders at bay, but in the fifth century the Western Empire was overrun. The Eastern Empire survived – just.

Constantius visits Rome
Here the Christian Emperor Constantius II, son of Constantine, enters Rome in AD 357. Although Emperor for many years, he had never seen the ancient capital; he was too busy defending the frontiers. Rome itself now had massive walls. The Germans sometimes broke through into Italy. The forts and the soldiers of the late Empire looked more medieval than Roman.

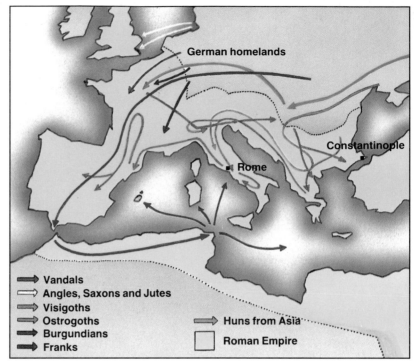

German homelands

Constantinople

Rome

⟹ Vandals
⟹ Angles, Saxons and Jutes
⟹ Visigoths
⟹ Ostrogoths
⟹ Burgundians
⟹ Franks

⟹ Huns from Asia
☐ Roman Empire

DATECHART

AD 230s onward Wars with Persia. Barbarian invasions across Rhine and Danube.

258 Western provinces break away to form the Gallic Empire.

271 Palmyra in Jordan revolts and seizes the Eastern Empire.

272-74 Aurelian reconquers the East, Gaul and Britain.

284-305 The reign of Diocletian.

303-311 Persecution of the Christians.

306 Civil wars.

311 Edict of toleration of Christianity.

324 Constantine becomes sole emperor.

325 Council of Nicaea.

361-3 Julian, last pagan Emperor.

395 Empire permanently divided.

406 Barbarians invade Gaul.

410 Visigoths capture Rome.

c410 End of Roman rule in Britain.

410-450 Western provinces fall to Germans.

451 Huns defeated.

475-476 Romulus Augustulus, last Emperor of the West.

527 Justinian Emperor of the East.

Desperate times

The third century was a dark time for many provinces, especially those near the frontiers. They were often overrun by foreign armies. Worse, they had to support the defending Roman armies – which also fought each other! Here some soldiers are taking supplies from a farm without paying. They are from a regiment chasing barbarian raiders who have set fire to another farm in the distance. Things like this bankrupted many farmers. Many became brigands, and a great deal of land was deserted.

Rough justice

From AD 212 almost everyone in the Empire was a Roman citizen, but this did not mean everyone was equal. The gap between rich and poor widened. Poor farmers were crushed by the weight of tax and rent. The wealthy could reduce them to a state little better than slavery. Right, a powerful landowner takes a tenant to court for non-payment of rent. There was no equality even in court; the poor could be tortured to gain evidence.

Brother Emperors

When Diocletian came to the throne he knew that it was no longer possible for one man to govern the Empire. He appointed three co-rulers. This is depicted in the statues, shown in the photograph, carved in the walls of St. Mark's in Venice. Henceforth, there were usually at least two emperors at a time.

The Christian Empire

Constantine became a Christian early in his reign. He lavished wealth on the Church, which soon became an important power. But it was divided by disputes over what was true belief. Constantine intervened. His bishops met at the Council of Nicaea in AD 325 (below) and reached a compromise. However, divisions remained, and sometimes broke out into violence. Christians also began to persecute pagans, as they had been persecuted.

Collapse of the West
Soon after AD 400, the Western Empire crumbled. Germans poured into Gaul. The Goths invaded Italy, and took Rome. Below, the proud aristocrats of Rome are forced to give their riches to the Gothic king, Alaric. But there was worse to come when the savage Huns swept west from central Asia, ravaging all in their path. Under such pressures, the West disintegrated. In AD 476, the last Western Emperor was deposed.

Survival of the East
The Germans set up their own kingdoms in the old Western provinces of the Empire, but neither they, nor the Persians, could conquer the much stronger Eastern Empire.

The Greek-speaking East had lost the ancient capital, but still thought of itself as the *Roman* Empire. It controlled many of the richest provinces, in Turkey, Syria and Egypt, and had the wealth to keep a big army to defend its frontiers.

While the German peoples fought each other for lands in the West, Rome lived on in the East.

The new Rome

Constantinople, the modern Istanbul, was founded by Constantine as his new capital in AD 330. Unlike Rome, it was from the start a Christian city and was adorned with beautiful churches, the greatest of which was Hagia Sophia (right). One of the great cities of the world, it stood at an important natural junction where the main road from Europe to Asia crossed the Bosporus, the channel linking the Mediterranean and the Black Sea. Its huge walls kept the East safe from the Germans.

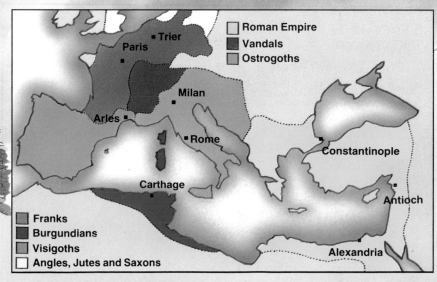

Roman Empire
Vandals
Ostrogoths

Franks
Burgundians
Visigoths
Angles, Jutes and Saxons

Trier
Paris
Milan
Arles
Rome
Constantinople
Carthage
Antioch
Alexandria

The Roman world in AD 525 Europe is a shifting pattern of German states. Rome is still strong in the East, and can resist both the Germans and the Persians.

New states appeared on the ruins of the old Western Roman Empire. They were to become the ancestors of the modern countries of Western Europe. Modern languages such as French, Spanish and Italian grew from Latin, and many countries still use the Latin alphabet.

The Eastern Empire did not fall. It lived on, but was soon very different from the old empire of Rome, even though it was its direct descendant and still called itself "Roman." We call it the Byzantine Empire. It gave much of the Greco-Roman heritage to Russia and Eastern Europe.

Byzantium lasted for another 1,000 years, and the final fall of its capital, Constantinople, to the Turks in 1453 was still within living memory when Columbus reached America in 1492.

Inspiration from the past
The memory of Rome is still powerful. The men who drew up the constitution of the United States knew Roman history, and were influenced by it. Words such as "constitution," "republic," "senate" and "capitol" are all taken directly from Rome. Classical architecture has also been reborn in recent centuries. It was used, for example, in designing the Capitol in Washington, DC, shown in the photograph.

The French Empire

Rome also influenced Napoleon Bonaparte. He called himself Emperor and his empire was modeled on Rome. The photograph (right) of a painting by David shows Napoleon crowning his Empress. The memory of Napoleonic glory is to be seen today on the Arc de Triomphe in Paris (below), which was built as a copy of a Roman triumphal arch (right).

From Byzantium to Russia

The Greek-speaking Christian Byzantine Empire has left its own legacy. This photograph of St. Basil's in Moscow shows the Byzantine influence on architecture. Byzantium greatly influenced the development of Russia and other Eastern European states, just as the Western Empire influenced Western Europe. Both the East and the West share common roots in the Empire of Rome.

INDEX

Photographic Credits:
Page 9: Mansell Collection; page 15: J. Allan Cash; page 16: Photosource; page 21: John Cleare; pages 22 and 27: Scala; pages 29 and 31 (center): Zefa; pages 30 and 31 (bottom): Greg Evans; page 31 (top): Bridgeman Art Library.